The Invisible Heart Strings

The Invisible Heart Strings

Bertrand Small

To all the members of my family son, daughter, brothers, sisters and mother and Father.

I extend my heartfelt gratitude to all who have shaped my journey, beginning on the picturesque Caribbean island of Antigua where I was born on May 9, 1968. As the youngest of five boys, I was fortunate to grow up in a close-knit family that instilled in me the values of love and resilience.

My father, whose guidance during my formative years steered me towards a career in technology, and my mother, who nurtured my dreams and aspirations, remain my greatest inspirations. Their loss, alongside the passing of my older brother and sister in 2017 and 2022 respectively, has deeply affected me, yet also propelled me to seek greater meaning in life and to honor their memories through my actions.

To all those who have inspired and supported my mission to spread love and compassion, thank you for believing in the power of small acts of kindness to create meaningful connections and improve our communities.

Lastly, to everyone who reads my story, may you be inspired to cherish your unique paths and strive to leave a legacy of love and compassion.

Once upon a time, there was a little girl named Lily who was very

confused about love. She had heard the word many times - her

parents said they loved her, she loved her stuffed bear, and she

was told to love her family, friends, and even broccoli! But Lily

didn't quite understand what love really meant.

One night, Lily made a wish upon a star that she could truly understand the meaning of love. Suddenly, her stuffed bear, Teddy, came to life! "Love isn't just a feeling, Lily," said Teddy. "It's much more than that. Let me show you."

Teddy directed Lily's gaze to her mother baking cookies in the kitchen. "See those invisible strings making shapes between you and your mom?" Lily looked closely and saw glistening strands connecting her and her mother's chests. "Those are heart strings," explained Teddy. "They show that you love each other through your caring actions."

Lily watched as more heart strings appeared when her mother gave her a warm hug. She saw them stretching between her dad and herself when he played her favorite game with her later that evening. Even her dog's loving licks at her feet created new strings.

"Love is about making choices to care for others through your actions," said Teddy. "The more you give your time, effort, patience, and kindness, the more those heart strings are strengthened between you and those you love."

From then on, Lily paid close attention to how many new heart strings she could create each day through caring acts big and small. When she shared her toys, helped with chores, or gave someone a hug, she pictured those invisible strings glowing brighter between their hearts.

At bedtime, she would count all the heart strings that connected her to her loved ones, glowing like brilliant Christmas lights from all the times she helped, considered others, and showed compassion throughout the day. Lily realized that real love wasn't just about nice feelings, but about persisting in caring deeds no matter what.

With Teddy's wisdom, Lily now understood that love is like an

invisible web that grows stronger every time we treat others

with kindness, respect, and selflessness. The more we nurture

those strands through positive actions, the more radiantly love

shines in our lives and the lives of those around us.

The next day, as Lily woke up, she felt a newfound purpose. Eager to see the magic of heart strings, she began her day by making her bed without being asked. She noticed a soft glow emanating from her chest to her bedpost. "Is this a heart string for myself?" she wondered.

Teddy, who had now become her constant companion, nodded. "Yes, Lily. Loving yourself is just as important. When you take care of yourself, you also create heart strings."

At school, Lily shared her crayons with a classmate who had forgotten theirs. She saw a thin, shimmering string form between them. "Thank you, Lily," said her classmate with a warm smile. Lily felt a pleasant warmth in her heart, and the string grew brighter.

During recess, she saw a child sitting alone, looking sad. Remembering Teddy's words, she approached and invited them to join her game. As they laughed and played together, Lily saw a beautiful string connecting them, vibrant and strong.

When she got home, she helped her mom set the table for dinner and listened intently to her dad's stories about his day at work. Each act of kindness and attention added more glowing strings, creating a beautiful web around her family.

That evening, as she lay in bed, Teddy spoke gently, "Lily, do you see how your actions today have created so many heart strings? These strings show the love and care you have shared with others. Love isn't just a feeling; it's a choice we make every day to be kind, patient, and selfless."

Lily nodded, feeling proud of the invisible web she had woven. She knew that even on days when she felt sad or tired, choosing to care for others would always light up her heart with glowing strings.

The next morning, inspired by her newfound understanding, Lily decided to spread love beyond her immediate circle. She baked cookies with her mom and delivered them to her elderly neighbor, who lived alone. The joy and gratitude in the neighbor's eyes added another brilliant string to Lily's collection.

She wrote a kind note to her teacher, thanking them for their hard work and dedication. The teacher's surprised and joyful reaction made Lily's heart swell with warmth, as yet another string was formed

Weeks turned into months, and Lily's web of heart strings grew.
She noticed that even the smallest acts, like smiling at a stranger
or picking up litter in the park, could create heart strings. She
realized that her actions could inspire others to do the same,
creating a ripple effect of love and kindness.

Lily's story spread through her community, and soon, others began to follow her example. The invisible web of heart strings extended beyond her family and friends, reaching neighbors, classmates, and even strangers. The town became a brighter, happier place as more and more people chose to act with love and kindness.

And so, Lily's simple wish upon a star transformed not only her understanding of love but also her entire community. She learned that love is an action, a choice we make every day. By nurturing and strengthening those invisible heart strings through our actions, we can create a world filled with radiant, glowing love.

Author Information

I was born on May 9, 1968, in Antigua, a picturesque Caribbean island. As the youngest of five boys, I grew up in a close-knit family. Unfortunately, I lost my father in my twenties, my mother the same year my daughter was born, and my older brother and sister in 2017 and 2022, respectively.

As a child, I dreamed of becoming a pilot. However, the high cost of education made this dream unattainable. Recognizing my passion for hands-on work, my father encouraged me to pursue computer skills during the era when graphical user interfaces were emerging.

My fascination with computers grew, leading to a career in technology. For over two decades, I specialized in computer and photocopier technology, receiving training at the highest levels from IBM and Canon. My expertise and dedication made me a respected professional in my field.

Despite my successful career, my quest to understand and teach the true meaning of love became a central part of my life. Inspired by personal losses and driven by a desire to make a positive impact, I focused on nurturing heart strings through acts of kindness and teaching others to do the same.

My life is marked by a commitment to spreading love and kindness. I strive to inspire those around me to create meaningful connections and improve their communities.

Through my actions and teachings, I aim to leave a legacy of love and compassion, encouraging others to make the world a better place.

My journey from aspiring pilot to technology expert and advocate for love and kindness showcases my resilience, passion, and dedication. My biography serves as an inspiration to cherish unique paths and spread love through everyday actions.